THE MONTGOMERY BUS BOYCOTT

A HISTORY PERSPECTIVES BOOK

Martin Gitlin

Published in the United States of America by Cherry Lake Publishing
Ann Arbor, Michigan
www.cherrylakepublishing.com

Consultants: Ibram H. Rogers, PhD, Assistant Professor, Africana Studies
Department, University at Albany, SUNY; Marla Conn, ReadAbility, Inc.
Editorial direction: Red Line Editorial
Book design and illustration: Sleeping Bear Press

Photo Credits: Montgomery County Sheriff's Office/AP Images, cover (left),
1 (left), 8; AP Images, cover (middle), cover (right), 4, 16, 17, 19, 30; Dick
DeMarsico/Library of Congress, cover (right), 1 (right); Horace Cort/AP Images, 7,
13, 24; Gene Herrick/AP Images, 10; Paul Cannon/AP Images, 12; Library of
Congress, 20; John Lent/AP Images, 22; Harold Valentine/AP Images, 29

Library of Congress Cataloging-in-Publication Data
Gitlin, Martin.
  The Montgomery bus boycott / Martin Gitlin.
    pages cm. – (Perspectives library)
  ISBN 978-1-62431-418-6 (hardcover) – ISBN 978-1-62431-494-0 (pbk.) –
ISBN 978-1-62431-456-8 (pdf) – ISBN 978-1-62431-532-9 (ebook)
1. Montgomery Bus Boycott, Montgomery, Ala., 1955-1956–Juvenile literature.
2. African Americans–Civil rights–Alabama–Montgomery–History–20th century–
Juvenile literature. 3. Civil rights movements–Alabama–Montgomery–History–
20th century–Juvenile literature.
4. Montgomery (Ala.)–Race relations–Juvenile literature. I. Title.
F334.M79N434 2013
323.1196'073076147–dc23
                    2013008487

Cherry Lake Publishing would like to acknowledge the work of
The Partnership for 21st Century Skills. Please visit *www.p21.org*
for more information.

Printed in the United States of America
Corporate Graphics Inc.
July 2013
CLFA11

TABLE OF CONTENTS

In this book, you will read about the Montgomery bus boycott of 1955 and 1956. Each perspective is based on real things that happened to real people who took part in or experienced the effects of the boycott. As you'll see, the same event can look different depending on one's point of view.

1

Reginald Brown
Church Leader

December 1, 1955, was a huge day for us. It was the beginning of the mass bus **boycott** in our city, Montgomery, Alabama. In Montgomery, buses are **segregated**. It all started because Negroes are allowed to sit only in the back rows of the bus. Most of us get up and stand if the seats in front reserved for whites fill up and a white person wants to sit down.

On that December day, Rosa Parks sat in a seat toward the back of a full bus. When a white man entered the bus, the bus driver asked Parks to give her seat to him. She refused and was arrested.

I know that Rosa Parks was not the first brave Negro in this fight for equality. So many people laid the groundwork for this boycott. Individuals such as Pastor Vernon Johns and organizations such as the Women's Political Council had wanted to do something about bus segregation before this day. Others were even arrested for protesting where Negroes could sit. But Parks's arrest was the spark that inspired us to take action against segregation in our community. Hallelujah for that **instrumental** day!

E. D. Nixon played a big role in the beginning of the bus boycott. He was Parks's supervisor at the Montgomery branch of the National Association for the Advancement of Colored People (NAACP). After her arrest, Nixon picked Parks's case to test bus

THE CHALLENGE FROM PASTOR JOHNS

Vernon Johns was a civil rights pioneer and a mentor to Martin Luther King Jr. and Ralph Abernathy. He was the pastor at the Dexter Avenue Baptist Church before King. Johns gave fiery sermons about oppression and segregation. He called on African Americans to take action to gain their civil rights. He once got off a bus and demanded a refund to protest bus discrimination. He also demanded service at a whites-only restaurant in Montgomery.

segregation. He knew she had enough courage and honesty to do it.

If it weren't for Nixon, I wouldn't be standing here smiling today. After Parks's arrest, he bailed her out of jail. Then he called church leaders like myself

African Americans could sit only in the backs of buses due to bus segregation.

for support. He set up a meeting on December 2 at the Dexter Avenue Baptist Church. At this meeting we planned to boycott the buses on Monday, December 5. Ralph Abernathy, pastor at my church, helped spread the word that all Negroes should not ride the bus that day. I called everyone I knew and told them not to ride the bus on December 5.

It wasn't only Negroes who wanted to stop bus segregation. Robert Graetz, a white pastor, backed our plan. He said he would advise his Trinity Lutheran

Church congregation to take part in the boycott.

On December 5, about 90 percent of Negroes who were regular passengers refused to ride the buses. I was so proud. I was proud of my church. I was proud of my fellow Negroes in Montgomery. I sensed that we were on our way to living out our belief that all people are created equal.

That day of the boycott, a few of us church leaders created the Montgomery Improvement Association to coordinate the boycott. We named Reverend Martin Luther King Jr. as its president. That evening, we held a meeting at the Holt Street Baptist Church. The meeting had been advertised over the weekend, and about 7,000 people packed into the church. Reverend King spoke and gave us courage to continue the boycott.

Toward the end of the meeting, Reverend Abernathy read a resolution to continue the boycott. The resolution stated our demands in order for the boycott to end. We required that Negroes be treated politely on the buses; that seating be first-come, first-served; and that Negro drivers be hired for Negro routes. Until those requirements were met, we would not ride on the city buses.

SECOND SOURCE

▶ Find another source about the first meeting of the Montgomery Improvement Association. Compare the information there to the information in this source.

That was three months ago. There has been so much work to do, and we continue to have our hands full. My church is a center of activity. We keep our spirits up. We motivate our congregation to stay off the buses because we are fighting for equality. We hold meetings about the boycott in many of Montgomery's Negro churches to keep the boycott going strong. People always pack the churches.

I have been helping people get where they need to go without buses. We have thousands of people who must find alternative **transportation** or risk losing their jobs. I find people who volunteer their cars and their time. I coordinate pickups based on the time and place Negroes are leaving their homes or getting out of work. The system is working smoothly.

▲ *Despite setbacks and violence, African Americans continued to come together and boycott the buses.*

I am thankful many people have rides to their jobs. But I also thank God for those who have worn out the soles of their shoes walking miles when cars have not been available. They are true heroes. As they walk to their destinations, they sometimes have to hear white people shout terrible insults at them.

If not for the church, they and others might have grown too fearful of the forces acting against them. We all might have wanted to stop the boycott after Reverend King's house was bombed on January 30, 1956. We might have given up when, on February 22, a Montgomery County grand jury **indicted** our leaders for violating a law that barred boycotts without just cause.

But we haven't. We will continue organizing and fighting until we receive dignity and justice.

THINK ABOUT IT

▶ Determine the main point of this chapter and pick out two pieces of evidence that support it.

Matilda Lee

Opponent of the Boycott

I liked Rosa Parks. She used to shop often at my fabric store. Parks is a seamstress. She came in nearly every day for needles, thread, and cloth. She was always friendly to me and very polite. She'd greet me with "How you doing today, Matilda?" A lot of folks around here wouldn't give a Negro the time of day, but I always greeted her back.

I thought Parks understood the need to separate the Negroes and the whites in Montgomery. That's why I was so surprised when I read in the papers that she was arrested for refusing to give up her bus seat to a white man. Her action sparked a boycott of the Montgomery buses that has been going on for nine months. It is now August 1956, and I don't see an end to the boycott in sight.

▲ *During the boycott, Montgomery buses were sometimes nearly empty.*

Parks and the preacher Martin Luther King Jr. have energized the Negroes. The buses are empty and so are our stores. The Negroes used to ride the buses downtown to work and to shop, but no more. Negroes could still walk to our stores, but now they've also boycotted white-owned stores. I've lost about $1,000. Other merchants I've talked to have lost money as well. My uncle works for the bus company. He told me they're losing all kinds of money too. He also told me Negro taxi drivers have lowered their fares to match the cost of taking a bus.

I didn't figure the bus boycott would last this long. I heard about a bus boycott a couple years back in Baton Rouge, Louisiana, that ended in two weeks. Negroes were given some more seats but not the front ones. I wonder if we could just do that here in Montgomery.

THINK ABOUT IT

▶ Read this chapter carefully. What surprises you about this perspective? Discuss this with a friend or classmate.

WHITES FOR THE BOYCOTT

Not all white people in Montgomery were against the boycott. White civil rights activist Virginia Durr, who was a friend of Rosa Parks, supported the boycott. She and her husband, along with E. D. Nixon, bailed Parks out of jail after her arrest. Another white supporter was Juliette Morgan. White segregationists threatened her after she wrote the following to the *Montgomery Advertiser* in December 1955:

> It is hard to imagine a soul so dead, a heart so hard, a vision so blinded and provincial as not to be moved with admiration at the quiet dignity, discipline, and dedication with which the Negroes have conducted their boycott.

▲ *The ruling in* Brown v. Board of Education *soon allowed whites and African Americans to attend school together.*

Just two years ago, in 1954, the U.S. Supreme Court ruled in *Brown v. Board of Education* that Negroes should attend the same schools as whites. Soon Negroes will want to eat in the same restaurants and swim in the same public pools. This is Alabama. We've got a proud tradition of separating the races, and it has been just fine so far.

I don't think we should use violence to stop the boycott though. That's where I put my foot down. It's terrible that the preacher King got his house bombed back in January. I'm glad nobody was hurt. I guess some white folks thought they had to do something

▲ *Many whites in Montgomery wanted to keep the city segregated.*

to scare him off. But King isn't one to scare easily. He is still leading the boycott as strongly as ever.

The Negro boycotters are sticking together, but it seems like we're falling apart. Mayor William Gayle called for whites to ride the buses instead of their cars, but that didn't work. The bus company had to raise fares just to keep running. This boycott is causing big financial problems for lots of folks.

I want the boycott to end as soon as possible, preferably with Negroes getting more seats in their own section. But I need to think about my business too. If the boycott continues for much longer, I'm not sure I'll still have a store next year.

ANALYZE THIS

▶ Take a close look at the first two narratives in this book. How are they different? Can you find similarities between the two?

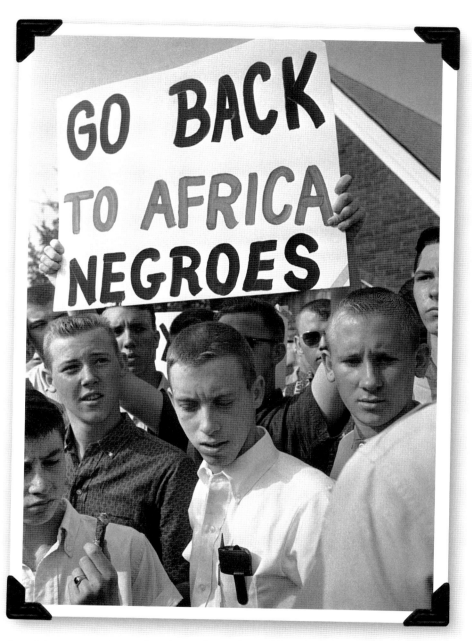

▲ *African Americans faced cruel words and harsh discrimination during the boycott.*

Louis Washburn

Civil Rights Activist

I couldn't be happier that Negroes can now ride alongside whites on Montgomery buses. Reaching this goal took a lot of time and planning many people don't even know about. For the bus boycott to work, Rosa Parks and a lot of other Negroes had to commit to the movement. But the boycott also required a lot more civil rights activists to continue leading the movement. Many of us worked behind the scenes to set up the boycott and keep momentum going.

Most folks know Rosa Parks is a seamstress who was arrested in December 1955 for refusing to give up her bus seat to a white man. But what many don't know is that she had been working as a secretary with us at the NAACP for quite some time. Our organization works to end racial segregation and discrimination wherever it exists. Before her arrest, Parks had finished a race-relations workshop at the Highlander Folk School in Tennessee.

So it was no accident that Parks acted that day in December. She had been involved in civil rights activities before, and she decided to act again. E. D. Nixon, our leader at the Montgomery branch of the NAACP, decided to use

ANALYZE THIS

▶ Find another chapter that discusses Rosa Parks. How are the two perspectives similar? How are they different?

▲ *E. D. Nixon played a key role in planning the Montgomery bus boycott.*

Parks's case to rally citizens to work toward ending bus segregation. His involvement in the boycott came at a price though. I'll never forget when his house was bombed on February 1, 1956. Luckily, no one was hurt.

Many other civil rights workers contributed greatly to the cause as well. One is Jo Ann Robinson. She was a professor at Alabama State College and president of the Women's Political Council. I recall Reverend Martin Luther King Jr. telling me Jo Ann was as active in the bus boycott as anyone was. She tried to get the Women's Political Council to start a protest against segregated buses years ago. Her members told her to forget it, that segregation was a fact of life in Montgomery. She refused to accept that. Her organization helped get the boycott started after Parks's arrest. Jo Ann distributed 35,000 flyers to Negroes around the area to urge them not to ride the buses.

Once the boycott began, we all had hard work to do. We had to organize transportation. Buses were the main way many of us got from place to place, so several people needed new means of transportation. I am not one who usually wakes up before dawn, but I did it for the cause. I am one of the few Negroes

▲ *Martin Luther King Jr. was one of the main leaders of the Montgomery bus boycott.*

in town who owns a car, so I drove it to the bus pickup station early in the morning and took people to their jobs. The transportation committee did a wonderful job. We found volunteers to drive 34 cars to 32 pickup spots from 5:30 a.m. to 12:30 a.m. About 30,000 people were taken to and from work every day.

Soon after the boycott began, Reverend King and Fred Gray gave the city a chance to stop the boycott. Gray was a civil rights activist with the Montgomery Improvement Association and one of two black lawyers in Montgomery. Gray and Reverend King issued reasonable demands on behalf of the Montgomery Improvement Association. We wanted polite treatment on buses; first-come, first-served seating; and Negro drivers to be hired for primarily Negro routes. The city commissioners rejected all the demands, and the boycott continued.

On February 1, 1956, Gray and fellow Montgomery Improvement Association attorney Charles Langford filed a lawsuit against bus segregation in the Federal District Court of Montgomery. I recall being in the barbershop on June 5, 1956, when a friend of mine

LEADER OF A MOVEMENT

The Montgomery bus boycott helped launch the civil rights movement of the 1950s and 1960s. Its leader, Martin Luther King Jr., went on to lead the struggle against racial segregation in Alabama and the rest of the country. He led the campaign that ended segregation of stores, restaurants, and schools in Birmingham. He also led the battle that gave African Americans voting rights throughout the South. For his work, he was awarded the Nobel Peace Prize in 1964. He continued his civil rights work until he was **assassinated** in 1968.

from the NAACP came rushing in. He was excited. He told me that the district court judges had ruled that bus segregation was a violation of the Fourteenth Amendment. This amendment guarantees all

American citizens equal rights under the law. I told him to sit down and get a haircut. I knew that the white leaders weren't going to let it go at that—and I was right. The court ruling was appealed by the city commissioners all the way to the Supreme Court.

When the case was appealed, we took it in stride and gathered our strength. We had been boycotting the buses for more than six months and it was getting easier every day. On November 13, 1956, the Supreme Court upheld the decision of the district court. Bus segregation was going to end! Mayor William Gayle tried to destroy the boycott until the very end. He had just issued a court **injunction** to stop Negroes from congregating on street corners while waiting for cars to pick them up.

SECOND SOURCE

▶ Find another source that discusses what life was like for African Americans during the Montgomery bus boycott. How does that information compare to what you read here?

The boycott continued for five weeks while the **mandate** that would force the bus company to integrate was processed. The boycott officially ended on December 20, and I got to sit in the front of the bus in time to do my holiday shopping. I could have driven, but I wanted to see the faces of my proud Negro brothers and sisters as they sat down in any open seat on the bus.

The forces of oppression are still strong, however. We continue to be harassed. The evil **Ku Klux Klan** tries to intimidate us with more bombs and by burning crosses in front of Negroes' homes. But we're no longer afraid. I saw one cross in flames with a young Negro boy near it warming his hands. I had to laugh.

There's more work to be done. I am more determined than ever—and so are my friends at the NAACP—to erase every trace of segregation in Montgomery. I plan on swimming in the same pools and eating in the same restaurants as the white citizens of this town one day—and hopefully soon.

▲ *King, second row left, and other African Americans rode in the front of the bus after Montgomery buses were desegregated.*

LOOK, LOOK AGAIN

This photo shows two African Americans riding in the front of a Montgomery bus in December 1956, the month the boycott ended. Use this image to answer the following questions:

1. How would a church leader describe this scene in a letter to a family member?

2. After seeing this scene, what would a person who was opposed to the boycott think?

3. How would a civil rights leader react after seeing this scene?

GLOSSARY

assassinate (uh-SAS-uh-nate) to murder someone who is well-known

boycott (BOI-kaht) a form of protest in which people refuse to buy goods or do business with someone

indict (in-DITE) to officially charge a person with a crime

injunction (in-JUNK-shuhn) a court order that prevents someone from doing something

instrumental (in-struh-MEN-tuhl) important; crucial

Ku Klux Klan (KOO KLUKS KLAN) an organization that promotes white supremacy and is known for violent actions against African Americans

mandate (MAN-date) a policy that must be carried out by elected officials

segregate (SEG-ri-gate) to separate or isolate a race or ethnic group from others, either by force or by discriminatory means

transportation (trans-pur-TAY-shuhn) a means for moving people and goods from one place to another

LEARN MORE

Further Reading

Ashby, Ruth. *Rosa Parks: Freedom Rider.* New York: Sterling, 2008.
Fleming, Alice. *Martin Luther King, Jr: A Dream of Hope.* New York: Sterling, 2008.
Freedman, Russell. *Freedom Walkers: The Story of the Montgomery Bus Boycott.* New York: Holiday House, 2008.

Web Sites

Eyes on the Prize: America's Civil Rights Movement 1954–1985
http://www.pbs.org/wgbh/amex/eyesontheprize/story/02_bus.html
This Web site has more information, videos, and images of the Montgomery bus boycott.

Rosa Parks Museum
http://trojan.troy.edu/community/rosa-parks-museum/
On this Web site, viewers can learn more about the Montgomery bus boycott and Rosa Parks.

INDEX

ABOUT THE AUTHOR

Marty Gitlin is a freelance writer based in Cleveland, Ohio. He has had about 70 educational books published, including many about American history. He has won more than 45 writing awards, including first place for general excellence from the Associated Press.